THE UNSEEN CITY

RARE AND UNUSUAL PHOTOGRAPHS OF WORCESTER

Worcester bridge on a very early photograph taken by Latham. Circa 1868.

THE UNSEEN CITY

RARE AND UNUSUAL PHOTOGRAPHS OF WORCESTER

RAY JONES

PARKBARN

COPYRIGHT 1998
RAY JONES

First published in Great Britain in 1998 by
Parkbarn
Martingale Cottage, Church Lane, Hallow, Worcester WR2 6PF

All rights reserved. No part of this publication may be
reproduced, stored in a retrieval system or transmitted, in any form
or by any means, electronic, mechanical, photocopying, recording or otherwise, without the prior
permission of the publisher.

ISBN I 898097 04 6

Typeset by Ray Jones in New Baskerville
Originally designed by John Baskerville a Worcestershire man in circa 1750
Printed by Severnside Pioneer Printers,
Upton-upon-Severn, Worcestershire.

Cover design by Ray Jones based on an Edwardian art nouveau postcard by Gaston Noury.

INTRODUCTION

All of the postcards and photographs reproduced in this book are from my own personal archive. Most of them have not, to my knowledge, been published before and hopefully therefore they offer the reader new insights into Worcester's recent past. The earliest photograph dates from the 1860s while most of the material represents the earlier years of this century. As far as possible I have tried to attribute individual photographs to the early local pioneers of photography but I still have much research to do in this area. A guide to our early photographers can be found below.

The photographs are presented in the form of an informal ramble through Worcester - starting in the city centre and touring around the river and outer suburbs. A number of social history photographs are also included as well as a quick look at Worcester's disappearing rural surrounds.

Background information has been drawn from many sources although special mention must be made of Michael Grundy's excellent *Memory Lane*. Peter Richardson was also extremely helpful with regard to the various Worcester Rowing Club photographs. Sometimes information I have concerning individual photographs is scanty and anything you can add to my knowledge would be welcome.

A. & G. Colwell - George Colwell, Greenhill Villa, London Road.
W. W. Dowty - William W. Dowty - No. 8 Broad Street (1916-1956).
Earl - F. C. Earl, No. 46 Broad Street.
Empire Studio - No. 4 Bridge Street.
Foy - J. Parkes Foy, No. 57 The Tything.
Max Fischer - No. 10 Barbourne Road & No. 33 Lowesmoor.
Franklin - No. 7 Green Hill, London Road.
W. W. Harris - Walter W. Harris, No. 101 High Street.
Homer - E. J. Homer, No. 60 Chestnut Walk.
P. Hutchison - Avon Studio, Cowl Street, Evesham.
Iliffe - Henry Iliffe, No. 38 High Street & No. 57 The Tything.
Pitt & Son - Jane Pitt & Son, 2, Park Avenue.
Percy Parsons - St Nicholas Street, No. 4 College Street, and No. 13 Summer Street.
T. Bennett & Sons - Thomas Bennett & Sons, No. 8 Broad Street (1879-1916).
A. Whinfield - Arthur H. Whinfield.

Bogie. Pet of the Smithin family, The Hill, Norton around 1910 and photographed by W. W. Harris. Published in memory of Winston (1981-1998).

PARKBARN PHOTOGRAPHIC ARCHIVE

Comprises:
Real and printed photographs of Worcester, Hallow, Grimley, Holt, Shrawley, Witley, Witley Court, Abberley, Clifton-On-Teme, Martley, Knightwick, Broadwas, Broadheath, Rushwick, Leigh Sinton, Alfrick, Suckley, Bransford, Powick, Callow End, Kempsey, Norton, Spetchley, Crowle, Fernhill Heath, Ombersley and areas around. Real photographic rural scenes including hop growing and market gardening.

The 237 photographs in this book have all been drawn from my own archive which consists of over 1,000 images of Worcester and over 1,500 images of the surrounding rural areas. I am planning to make these available for reproduction to the public at large and if you are interested in obtaining good quality photographs for reference, framing, presents and the like then please register your requirements with me. I am also anxious to purchase new material and will pay good prices for interesting postcards and photographs. As a member of the Postcard Traders Association I am always willing to advise on any accumulations of postcards you may have whether they be local, British, or foreign.

Please contact:
Ray Jones, Martingale Cottage, Church Lane, Hallow, Worcester WR2 6PF.
Telephone 01905 - 640014

OTHER PARKBARN PUBLICATIONS

Worcester in Recent Times by Bill Meadows and Geoffrey Hopcraft - both well-known local photographers of repute. Bill and Geoff's first photographic look at Worcester contains 231 photographs of Worcester encompassing the period from the late 1940s to the early 1980s. Priced at £11.95.

Porcelain in Worcester 1751-1951: An Illustrated Social History by Ray Jones BA. Comprising 95 A4 pages containing 163 photographs and illustrations. An essential book for anyone interested in the history of porcelain manufacture in Worcester. Priced at £9.95.

Worcester's Lost Theatre - The Story of the Worcester Theatre Royal by Suz Winspear. 120 A4 pages containing 46 illustrations and photographs. A fascinating story that is of interest to both local residents familiar with Worcester's past, and theatre buffs eager to learn more about the origins of provincial theatre history. Priced at £13.95.

Around Worcester in Old Photographs by Ray Jones BA. Contains over 200 black & white photographs. Published by Sutton Publishing. Priced at £3.99 (new lower price).

Worcestershire at Work by Ray Jones BA. Contains around 200 black & white photographs. Published by Sutton Publishing. Priced at £3.99 (new lower price).

These books can be ordered directly from Parkbarn or obtained from good local bookshops.

386-8   Cross & St. Nicholas Church, Worcester.

1 A familiar view of the Cross but with a flavour of the 1930s seldom seen on postcard views. This series was published for Miss C. Fortey who was a tobacconist at No. 14 Foregate Street.

2 A rare view of the coronation celebrations in 1911. The fine building occupied by the London City and Midland Bank is now a branch of the Nationwide Building Society. Postally used on 8 September 1911.

THE CROSS   WORCESTER.

7

3 Broad Street looking away from the Cross. Postcard not postally used but dating from the 1920s. R. A. Roberts, the tailors, entice shoppers inside with their 'new patent secret inside sleeve pocket'.

4 The premises of Albert E. Marshall, dispensing chemist, of No. 59 Broad Street. Postcard sent by the owner as a Christmas greeting but unfortunately is undated. Marshall is listed in Littlebury's directory for 1908, but by 1916 he had been replaced by Sidney Charles Wallis, photographer. The TSB Bank now occupies this building.

5 An unusual view of the Crown Hotel - part of an advertising postcard from the Edwardian period when the Misses Halbeard were proprietresses.

6 An advertising postcard that probably dates back to the 1920s.

7 Another extract from an advertising postcard featuring the Gloucestershire Furnishing Co., who were based at Nos. 52/53 Broad Street. The postcard was used by a member of staff on 24 July 1907 and addressed to the Crown Inn in Bransford Road, St Johns.

9

8 The corner of Bank Street and High Street, probably around 1930. To the left is the store of Simes the drapers. Lloyds Bank dominates the corner of Bank Street. Between Lloyds and the Cross are the well-known premises of J. W. Cassidy & Son Ltd. (watchmakers); Dick's Central Boot Stores; and the Midland Bank.

9 A rare postcard view of Lady Huntingdon's Free church, postally used on 25 April 1904.

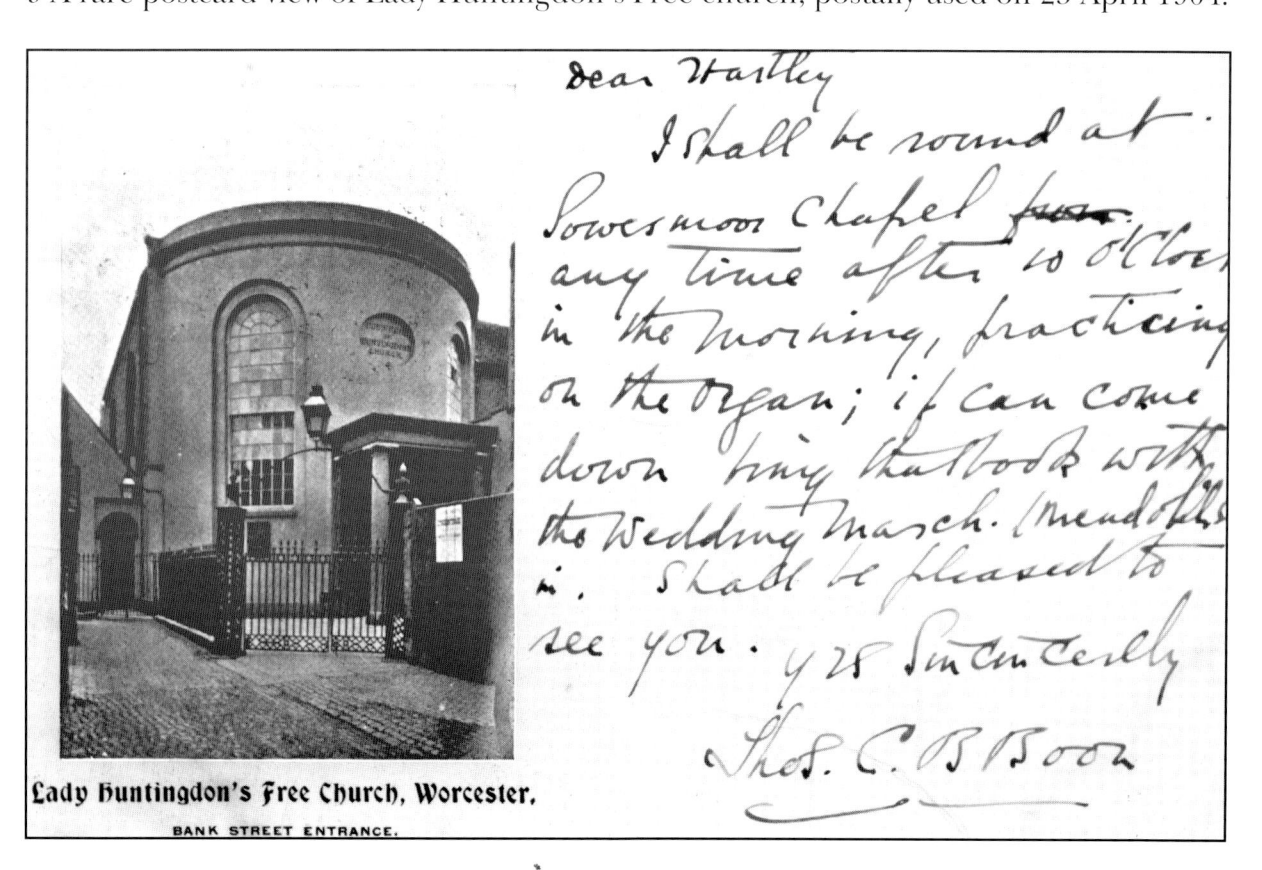

10 Simes drapery stores as decorated for the coronation celebrations of 1911. Postcard sent by an employee to her friend on 23 July 1911. Simes were still in business as late as the outbreak of World War II but had been replaced by Bobby & Co. Ltd. by 1955. This is now the site of Debenhams.

11 Interior view of Shuter & Flay's Stores who were family grocers at Nos. 51 & 52 High Street. This postcard was sent by the store to customers to inform them of their representative's next call. They were still in business as late as 1955 with their neighbours being Littlewoods and David Greig Ltd. They were thus at the heart of the central business district.

12 & 13 Processions in Edwardian times appear to have been a regular occurrence but the reason for them is not always obvious. Fortunately the 'Berrows Illustrated Supplements' sometimes provide the solution. The edition of 29 May 1909 states that the real photographic postcard (above) is the Empire Day Parade - the mayor and citizens, and Territorials parade to the Cathedral. The facade of the market hall can be seen to the right. (Percy Parsons) Below is a similar procession with the banner of the Order of Oddfellows prominent. Berrows (15/10/10) states that this is the Oddfellows Centenary Church Parade. (Max Fischer)

14 The Guildhall decorations for the 1911 coronation. Postally used on 26 July 1911.

15 A further view of the Guildhall decorations. The premises beyond the Guildhall are those of Charles W. Palmer (draper), while on the left 'Hills' would have been the premises of Albert Hills (a boot & shoe warehouse). Postally used on 18 July 1911.

16 A busy High Street scene. Beyond the Guildhall are the premises of Spark & Co. (music warehouse) and Georges Restaurant.

17 A court in Fish Street. The construction of Deansway irrevocably changed the character of this street. (Postcard produced from 1886 engraving by F. S. Bayley)

18 Pump Street Methodist church. I understand that it was demolished in 1901 although the postcard was not postally used until 26 October 1907. (A. & G. Colwell)

19 Another procession, this time pictured at the junction of High Street and College Street. Postally used on 30 May 1910. The Berrow's Illustrated Supplement (28/05/10) states that this is the late King's Memorial Service. (A. & G. Colwell)

20 The Mayor's Procession en route to the Cathedral in December 1913. The writer claims to be looking for a sixpenny piece at the time of the snapshot which was taken by Max Fischer.

15

21 Friar Street - the old. A rare postcard view that probably dates back to the 1890s and could well be one of T. Bennett & Sons early archive photographs reproduced in postcard format.

22 Another early Friar Street view looking south, circa 1906. From the left are the premises of William Rowberry, fried fish shop; Ernest John Goodwin, hardware dealer; a fruiterer's shop; then there is a narrow entrance leading into George's Yard - a typical court housing glovers, carpenter, labourers etc.; Henry Waldron, china rivetter; Ruth Waldron, umbrella repairer. (W. W. Harris)

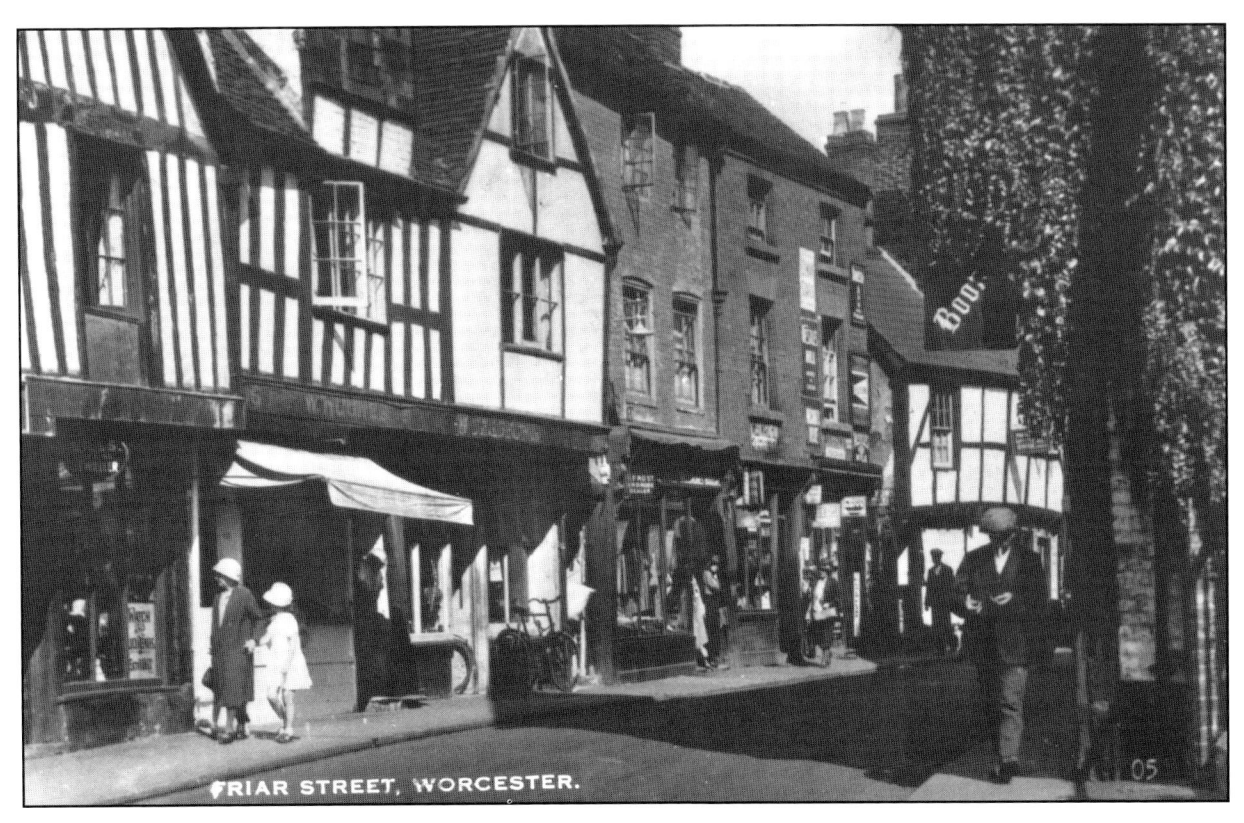

23 A 1930s view of Friar Street showing the premises of (from left to right) Ernest Giles, watchmaker; William Hughes, butcher; -?-; Mrs Alice Frost, wardrobe dealer; William McHarg, hairdresser; and George F. Collins, shopkeeper.

24 A Friar Street court. On the opposite side of the street is the premises of Thomas Frost, wardrobe dealer. (W. W. Harris)

25 The premises of C. Jones (one of many butchers in the Shambles). To the left is the aptly named Butchers Arms. (F. S. Bayley)

26 The Tudor Coffee House. Situated at Nos. 38, 40 & 42 Friar Street. Circa 1916 when Miss Fanny Davies was manageress.

27 The Hartlebury VAD Hospital arranged occasional visits for its convalescents. A party from the hospital is viewed outside the Lasletts Almhouses on 12 November 1918. On brake - top row, left to right: the driver, Pte. Brady, Pte. Souster, Gnr. Dennison. Bottom row, Sgt. Clarke, Nurse Cox, Pte. Devenish, Nurse Gardner, Pte. Parker, Pte. Bullock. Standing, Gnr. Hunt, Gnr. Colclough, Pte. Mitchell, Commandant, Pte. Waller, Pte. Kent, Gnr. Gunn. Second brake, Sister, Pte. Elwood.

28 The inner courtyard of the Reindeer Hotel during the early Edwardian period. Postcard published by Burrow of Cheltenham and postally used on 19 January 1904. This view is easily recognised as part of the Reindeer Court development.

29 An advertising postcard depicting the staff and premises of A. Stiles & Son, No. 3 St Swithin Street. Postally used on 15 May 1909, the message reads, 'Please send pig in on Monday, May 17th'.

30 Yet another procession scene, probably one of the 'Civic Welcomes' held for the returning battalions of the Worcestershire Regiment at the end of the First World War. (W. W. Dowty)

31 The premises of E. J. Parsons, seed & bulb merchants who were situated at No. 18 St Nicholas Street. They were also situated at the Barbourne nurseries in Droitwich Road (formerly W. B. Rowe & Son and situated between The Blanquettes and Bilford Lane), and exhibited at various local shows (see photo No. 60). Parsons had formerly worked with Richard Smith & Co. Ltd. who had massive nurseries in St Johns.

32 Foregate Street looking northwards, circa 1912.

33 A busy Foregate Street scene on a postcard dated 5 July 1931. The tram tracks were torn up some two years earlier,

34 A funeral at St Nicholas's Church. Photograph by Homer and is supposedly the funeral of Mr & Mrs Laight's child. Unfortunately the postcard is undated.

35 A superb scene of the decoration of the Star Hotel in preparation for the coronation celebrations of 1911. Part of the decorations celebrate the British Empire - how times change - now we have to apologise for our colonial past!

36 A rare view of No. 20 Foregate Street in 1915 when it was the residence of a surgeon, Samuel Wellesley Coombs F.R.C.S., L.R.C.P. (Edinburgh). He would have had only a short stroll to post a letter being next door but one to the main post office. This building no longer exists having made way for the Gaumont Cinema.

37 Worcester Post Office on the corner of Foregate Street and Pierpoint Street. This is now the site of the Postal Order public house. This at least bucks the modern trend of naming public houses without any regard for local history and tradition. Postcard postally used on 21 July 1905.

38 The Victoria Institute on a postcard published by C. Fortey. Circa 1910.

39 Foregate Street beyond the railway bridge looking northwards. The post office shown in photo No. 37 can be seen on the right. The Gaumont Cinema was built during the 1930s but its heyday was probably during the 1960s when illustrious performers included the Beatles and the Rolling Stones.

40 Shire Hall pictured on a postcard postally used on 27 July 1906. A little changed scene though lacking the scaffolding of recent times.

41 Worcester Royal Infirmary as viewed from the north side of Castle Street. The similarity in architectural style with this building and Bevere House is no coincidence as both were designed by the eminent Gloucestershire architect, Anthony Keck. It was built in 1771 and replaced the original infirmary in Silver Street. The original infirmary still survives, albeit in a sorry state and half-hidden by more modern commercial neighbours.

42 Worcester Royal Infirmary as viewed from Pitchcroft. Postally used postcard dated 8 July 1908. On the left can be the seen the spires of the Presbyterian Christ church and St Mary's church.

43 North Quay looking northwards on 15 July 1919. This is probably a unique view of the 'Butts spur' railway line. Photo by J. B. Sherlock who specialised in railway views.

44 Southend United Football Club. Presumably the local, not the Essex, version pictured at Pitchcroft.

45 Mr Edward Lamb was Captain of Worcester Rowing Club from 1911-1913. He is pictured outside the clubhouse that sadly burnt down in recent times.

46 A fascinating photograph of an early steam launch on the Severn. The view would appear to be roughly opposite to the Rowing Club and those on board were probably members of the club. Definitely recognisable is Edward Lamb (third from left).

47 Worcester Rowing Club would appear to date back earlier than most of us would have thought! This prehistoric scene was captured by Percy Parsons and probably features a heavily disguised member of the Lamb family. Postcard sent by Percy Lamb (Edward's brother) to his sister on 10 July 1905.

48 Worcester Regatta in 1911. Edward Lamb, the new Captain, features prominently. The view is north of the clubhouse looking south. The main event was a one mile distance senior fours - the 'Toddington Challenge Vase & Corporation Plate' - which had a prize of four handsome cups and a coxwain's prize (total value £20).

49 The winners of the 'Saltford (Bath) Regatta - Freeman Challenge Vase' for maiden fours in 1913. Back row, left to right: F. Trietline, E. Lamb (captain), G. H. Gibbs. Sitting: R. H. Findon, R. Evans (cox), and P. White. This crew proved to be the most successful in the club's history at that time.

50 Worcester Regatta on 18 June 1914. This was the high diving exhibition which took place at the end of the paddock enclosure and was performed by members of the Amateur High Diving Association, London. Amongst their number was the champion of England between 1909 and 1912, Mr. H. E. Pott. (W. W. Dowty)

51 The annual regatta river trip in August 1929. A large party poses by the clubhouse before boarding the 'Belle'. Amongst the gathering are the Lamb brothers, Thomas and William Wyatt, Satan Collier, Charles Dimolene, and Rupert Newth. (E. J. Homer)

52 Pitchcroft was the usual scene of early aviation activity in Worcester. The first aeroplane seen in Worcester was possibly at the Herefordshire & Worcestershire Agricultural Show in June 1910. However the aeroplane was forced to swerve when manoeuvring through the crowd ending in a nasty accident resulting in the death of one unfortunate Hindlip lady. This is Colonel Cody, the renowned American pioneer, flying in August 1911. (Max Fischer)

53 F. W. Gooden, an early flying ace was a visitor to Pitchcroft on 23 July 1914. He performed the 'loop the loop' which was reported to be 'very decent'. (Empire Studio)

54 A close up view of F. W. Gooden aboard a Morane Saulniere 80 H.P. Gnome aircraft. This postcard would have been sold at all events Gooden appeared at up and down the country. (Topical Postcard Company, Winton, Hants)

55 An early aeroplane pictured at Pitchcroft on a postcard by the Empire Studio.

56 Another Pitchcroft early aviation view, this time taken by W. W. Dowty.

57 A later view which possibly features the flying trips that could be made from Pitchcroft for the princely sum of 5 shillings during the 1930s. Sir Alan Cobham and his 'Flying Circus' provided the aircraft.

58 Pitchcroft was the venue for Empire Day in 1917. In the far distance, on the left, can be seen the chimney of Spreckley's Brewery. (W. W. Dowty)

59 The Three Counties Show at Pitchcroft. The stand of Mann & Sons Ltd. They were a prominent High Street shop being next door to Shuter & Flays. Circa 1920.

60 The stand of Edward J. Parsons. Parsons (see photo No. 31) had rapidly expanded his own business and regularly exhibited at other local shows such as Madresfield. Circa 1920.

61 The Dog & Duck Ferry. A pleasant way to cross the Severn. In the late 1950s, when my family lived in Vine Street, I remember my father taking me on this ferry in order to visit my grandparents who lived in Church Walk, off Tybridge Street. On the right is an advertisement hoarding for R. A. Roberts & Co. who were tailors at No. 32 The Cross (see photo No. 3). Circa 1910.

62 The opposite side of the ferry. A real photographic postcard taken by Percy Parsons who postally used it himself on 5 September 1931.

63 An early view of Gheluvelt Park on a postcard published by Cockerton's of the Ombersley Road Post Office (proprietor was Frederick A. Cockerton). The original post office for this area was at the corner of Perdiswell Street and Ombersley Road (now Johnsons Newsagents).

64 A later view of Gheluvelt Park. Postcard postally used in 1953.

65, 66 & 67 Three views of the old water tower that used to exist to the north of Gheluvelt Park, close to the Severn. It was of eighteenth century origin and had an elevated water tank. Water from the Severn was pumped into the tank via a waterwheel which then flowed by means of a gravitational process to the main water works in the Trinity.

68 Kepax Ferry looking north, circa 1936. Maybe the time is ripe to re-introduce our largely long lost ferries. How about a park & ferry service!

69 The advantages of a park & ferry service are not to be ignored. A tranquill way to travel accompanied by views such as the one below which shows the riverbank adjacent to the Kepax Ferry travelling north. The house in the background is Avenbury, once a nursing home and where your author was born! Postcard postally used on 2 May 1910.

70 Perdiswell Hall was built in 1787-8 for the well-known Wakeman family, who were a typical example of an affluent Georgian family involved in various local affairs and business. By the early 1900s the hall had changed hands several times but it was customary for the grounds to made available for public use as can be seen by the following photographs. (Pitt & Son)

71 St Martin's Fête was held in the grounds of Perdiswell Hall in September 1910. This was the 'Smelling competition - Guess the perfume - 17 goes for threepence.' (Max Fischer)

PRIMROSE LEAGUE FÊTE 1914 4

72 & 73 Perdiswell was also the venue for the Primrose League Fête of 1914. This was apparently organized by Malvoma, the tomato & cucumber specialist of Malvern. The postcard below came from the E. J. Parsons family postcard album (horticultural firm based at No. 18 St Nicholas Street). The Primrose League was a women's section of the Conservative Party which was initially, at least, sympathetic to the cause of women's suffrage. The grounds of Perdiswell Hall were used as an airfield during World War II while the house was used for billeting. Fire damaged the property in 1956 and it was then demolished. (Max Fischer)

74 Who needs park & ride? You need some traffic first! Droitwich Road looking north with Penbury Street on the left. This postcard is one of a series produced by a local photographer who sadly failed to acknowledge his own work in some form or another. Circa 1908.

75 The Raven, Droitwich Road, Claines. The proprietress is Mrs Tredwell. The 1908 entry in Littlebury's boasted of: 'Ales, Wines, Spirits and Cigars of the finest quality. Good accomodation for cyclists. Teas a speciality.' Incidentally the 1879 edition of Littlebury's lists James Collins as proprietor of the Raven at Claines with the location described as Red Hill.

76 A rare photograph of the premises of Charles Adams, timber merchant & wheelwright situated at No. 146 Ombersley Road. They were situated in the vicinity of the currently derelict Northwick Cinema (used as a bingo hall and entertainment venue in recent years).

77 Ombersley Road looking northwards away from the junction with Pinkett Street. The postcard was sent by the occupiers of Ivydene (the house furthest from the camera) and is dated 12 December 1907. At the time Pinkett Street was effectively the last side road on the left of the Ombersley Road (Beckitt's [sic] Lane being a rural backtrack leading to Northwick). On the righthand side, howevever, both Checketts Lane and Whinfield Road had considerable housing development.

78 Ombersley Road looking north towards the junction with Checketts Lane. Both photos Nos. 78 & 79 are from an unattributed photographer's series (see photo No. 74). Circa 1908.

79 Ombersley Road looking north from the vicinity of Checketts Lane. The advertising boards are those of the Claines Fruit & Vegetable Gardens (the proprietor was Francis Morris who was also a sand & gravel merchant as well as being a family butcher). Circa 1908.

80 A tram heads towards the city centre. Pictured at the junction of Perdiswell Street with Ombersley Road. The post office, just out of view, was run by Mrs S. E. Lambert in 1908.

81 Ombersley Road Wesleyan church. The railings were no doubt taken away to be melted down to make weapons during the war. In 1908 the other Wesleyan places of worship in Worcester were in Pump Street and Bromyard Road.

82 A rare photograph of the Free Masons of Worcester cart. Pictured possibly in the vicinity of Barbourne Bank, once the home of the Overall family who had masonic connections.

83 Barbourne Road looking towards the old toll house at the junction of Ombersley Road and Droitwich Road. In 1908 Henry Chamberlain, fly proprietor occupied the Droitwich Road side of the Toll House while Charles North, pianoforte tuner, was in residence on the Ombersley Road side.

84 A well attended outing prepares to leave the Swan Inn in Barbourne Road. The licensee in 1908 was John Sylvester Mayman. The Swan is also listed in the 1879 Littlebury's when William Henry Wall was licensee.

85 The left hand side of Somers Road as viewed from Lyttelton Street. Clare Villas are on the left while the ivy clad house is Ochil Villa. This view has little changed. Postcard postally used on 11 November 1908. (Max Fischer)

The Yew Secondary School, Worcester.

86 Captioned the Yew Secondary School (postcard postally used in 1942), this building has been the home to the City of Worcester Secondary School for Girls, Worcester Girls Grammar School, Bishop Perowne, and is now part of the Worcester College of Technology. The site was formerly occupied by Thames House.

87 Do you know where? Not an easy view to recognise but Max Fischer, the photographer, was looking northwards on the Barbourne Road, with his camera positioned in the vicinity of Shrubbery Avenue. Photograph taken during the snowstorms of January 1912. The school shown above was to be built on the left in the late 1920s.

88 Motor-cycle football at St Georges Lane. Probably a photograph from the late 1930s when crash helmets seemed an unnecessary encumbrance. *Memory Lane* featured this subject on 17 October 1998.

89 Spreckley's Brewery dominates this view of Barbourne Road looking southwards towards the city centre. This photograph probably dates from the early 1960s. I must say that Barbourne Road looks far smarter without the bus lane.

90 Members of the Upper Sixth of the Worcester Royal Grammar School in 1948. If my memory serves me correctly they are posed in front of the entrance to the Main Block. (Foy)

91 A traditional confectioner's shopfront situated at No. 46 The Tything. Miss Mabel L. Barton was the proprietress listed in Kelly's between 1924 and 1940. In the window is a poster advertising a Bridge Drive & Dance, in aid of the Worcestershire Girl Guides, at the Guildhall on the 1 February 1929.

92 An aerial view of the Alice Ottley School in the early 1960s. On the right are the St Oswalds Almshouses.

93 Elephants from the circus of Barnum & Bailey pass the Alice Ottley School on 3 November 1898. (A. Whinfield)

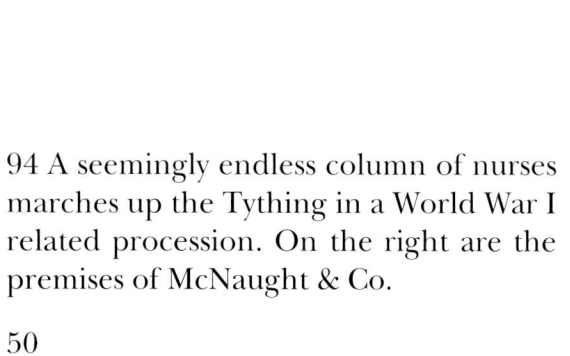

94 A seemingly endless column of nurses marches up the Tything in a World War I related procession. On the right are the premises of McNaught & Co.

95 Sansome Walk Band of Hope, circa 1910. They were founded in 1879. (A. & G. Colwell)

96 Postal staff outside the entrance to the sorting office in Sansome Walk. Only in recent times has this location changed.

97 & 98 Elephant & Castle, Sansome Walk. This public house was in the ownership of the Smith family for many years. In the photograph below a Smith family wedding party is shown outside the front of the pub. The building still survives although the pub does not, having closed its doors for the last time in the late 1960s.

99 & 100 The traditional public house is gaily decorated to celebrate the coronation of our Queen. The interior view below is of the aptly named 'Coronation Bar'. (W. W. Dowty)

53

101 & 102 Astwood Road premises of The Worcester New Co-operative & Industrial Society. The postcard to the right was postally used on 28 July 1912. In 1908 there were similar branches at No. 46 Barbourne Road; St. John's; and No. 17 Union Street. The main branch was situated at Nos. 6 & 8 St Nicholas Street. This location is opposite today's large store, being the corner of Trinity Street and St Nicholas Street nearest the Cross.

103 Mayfield Road in the early years of this century. Many of the residents at that time would have been involved in various aspects of railway work - guards, drivers, fitters, signalmen etc. (attributed to Max Fischer)

104 Astwood Road Cemetery entrance. Although this view is very different now the same stonework can still be seen in the wall of the cemetery along the Astwood Road. Incidentally I wonder how many of you have sent friends and relatives postcards illustrating cemeteries!

105 Astwood Halt - perhaps another candidate for park & ride. It closed on 25 September 1939. This view shows an LMS Stanier locomotive No. 5272 passing Astwood Halt on 30 June 1938. This was the Gloucester to Leicester service.

106 Worcester locomotive shed yard with Railway Walk - a favourite venue for train spotters over the years - in the background. They would no doubt have been interested by the appearance of John Owen (No. 1385) at Worcester, a locomotive originally from the Whitland & Cardigan Railway, but destined to finish its career at Worcester.

107 The view from Railway Walk in early 1914. On the left are the extensive sheds of the carriage and wagon repairing works, while on the extreme right are the main locomotive sheds. The church in the distance is that of the Holy Trinity.

108 Railway horses at Shrub Hill. Horses were regularly used on the Great Western Railway and one of the tasks for horses such as these was to haul goods from one platform to another. At Shrub Hill a level crossing for this purpose existed until 1909. At Hartlebury in 1909 they had the heaviest horse recorded, weighing in at one ton (Midland system, GWR).

109 A large elm butt removed from Hindlip and weighing 13 tons 5 cwt. Probably bought by Alfred Bevan Purnell, corn merchant, of No. 43 Lowesmoor.

110 Shrub Hill Road on a postcard sent on 28 November 1906. The familiar premises of Heenan & Froude (then known as the Shrub Hill engineering works) are on the left. Built in the 1860s as a locomotive and rolling stock construction works, its occupants, the Worcester Engine Works Co., went into liquidation in 1871. This fine Victorian building remained empty until 1882 when it was an ideal venue for the Worcestershire Exhibition. On the right are the premises of the South Wales & Cannock Chase Coal Company.

111 British School for Boys pictured on 10 May 1910. This is probably Class 2 and by chance I also have a photograph of Class 5 taken on the same day. The school was located at St Martin's Gate.

112 A rare view of Tallow Hill looking northwards. Today as you turn left over the hump-back bridge over the canal this would be roughly where the photographer (probably William Hooper of Swindon) took this shot. On the left is Cemetery Terrace, while framed by the tree is the Crown Inn. The tree stands within the grounds of the disused cemetery.

113 The Oddfellows Arms was situated at the corner of South Street with Carden Street. The owners were Spreckley's, the Worcester based brewers, and the landlord in 1908 was Thomas Henry Lippit whom I presume is shown in this photograph. This public house closed down on 30 May 1964. At one time there were 23 public houses within the Blockhouse area.

114 A strictly male outing leaves the Park Street Tavern in Little Park Street. Mrs Leah Blake was the licensee.

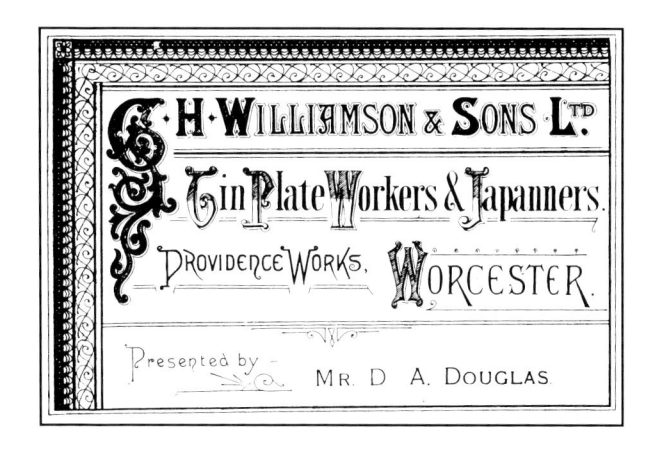

115 Representatives calling card for G. H. Williamson & Sons Ltd. Probably dating back to the early years of this century.

116 An unknown Williamson's driver poses by a Morris Commercial vehicle.

117 & 118 Two unusual views of workers at the Royal Porcelain Works. Dipping plates in glaze preparatory to firing is shown above. To the right is shown the handling process.

119 The Albion Flour Mills owned by T. S. Townshend & Sons Ltd. To the left can be seen the Royal Porcelain Works complete with long lost kilns. The site of the former china works of James Hadley & Sons (1896-1905) is directly behind the flour mills on the opposite side of the canal. The mills were eventually bought by the Worcester Royal Porcelain Co. but shortly afterwards, on 11 December 1960, a huge fire caused considerable structural damage.

120 Bath Road pictured at the junction with Diglis Road (formerly known as the Lower Bath Road). The Albion Inn is obscured by a tree. Trams left the Cross at half hourly intervals on the Bath Road route except on busy days such as Saturdays and Mondays when extra trams would run. There was no service on Sunday mornings. Postcard postally used on 2 May 1912.

121 An aerial view of the Dock Basin and Diglis looking towards the Bath Road. Probably a photograph taken in the 1930s.

122 & 123 Two unusual views of the Aston Saw-mills at Diglis Dock. Circa 1934. Walter H. Aston was an English & foreign timber merchant with 25,000 acres of forest at Kalvia, Finland.

124 Orchard Street, Cherry Orchard. This and the following two views appear to be part of a series of six postcards which probably date back to the 1920s. Cherry Orchard was a small housing development (Berwick Street, Stanley Street, Waverley Street, Cavendish Street and Orchard Street) surrounded by countryside in 1908 and was the terminus of the Bath Road tramway route. Nearby was Duck Brook farm.

125 Timberdine Avenue as seen from the Bath Road.

126 Barneshall looking towards the city centre. On the right is Bunns Road.

127 A rare, possibly unique, postcard of an early trackless car, built by Charles and Walter Santler, photographed at the Timberdine Oil Store owned by Bury's. The garage was situated on the Bath Road somewhere between Wheatfield Avenue and the Ketch Hotel. Santler & Co. were based at No. 2 Alma Villas, Worcester Road, Malvern Link. The car was apparently owned by Mr. Bury at that time (circa 1937).

128 The Lodge, Battenhall Mount, Battenhall Road. The residence of Major Chichester in 1908. (W. W. Harris)

129 Battenhall Mount. Home of the Honourable Alfred Percy Allsop (a member of the brewing family) when this photograph was taken (circa 1908). He was three times Mayor of Worcester - in 1892, 1894 and 1909 - and was a colourful member of local society. His good times, however, came to an end in 1913 when he was forced to file for bankruptcy. (Percy Parsons)

130 An interior view of the Mount when used as a VAD hospital between 1915-1919. Doctors responsible for the patients include Doctor Springer and Doctor Gostling. (W. W. Harris)

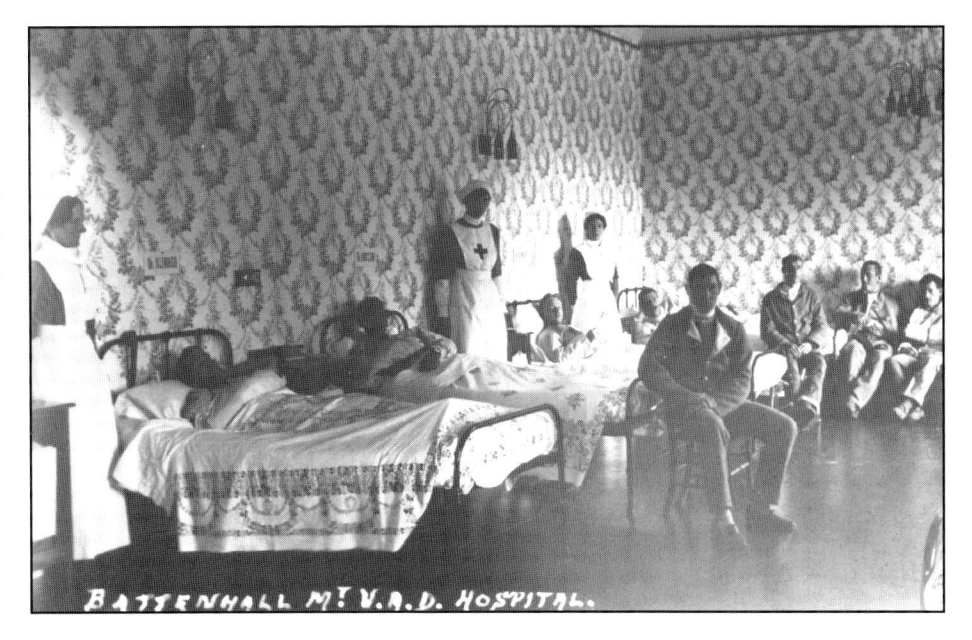

131 Recuperating soldiers in the grounds of Battenhall Mount. There were 72 beds available for the patients who were treated by staff who had freely volunteered their services. Apparently only the cook was paid so lets hope the food was satisfactory. (W. W. Harris)

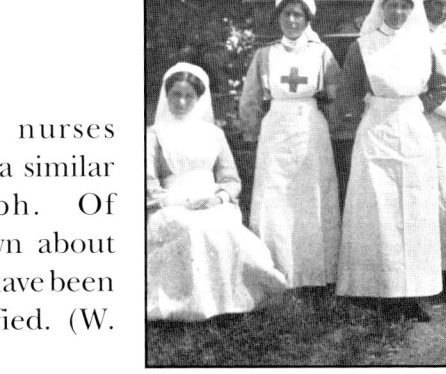

132 The nurses gather for a similar photograph. Of those shown about ten would have been fully qualified. (W. W. Harris)

133 Fort Royal Park and the Cathedral as seen in the 1930s. Fort Royal Park is older than Cripplegate Park and Gheluvelt Park, having opened in 1915. Fort Royal was the scene of much carnage in the Battle of Worcester fought in 1651.

134 London Road looking away from the city on a postcard postally used on 28 May 1909. Battenhall Road is on the right while the buildings on the left are Rose House and Rose Hill. The fine wall on the left still exists in part, although in rather in a decrepit state.

135 London Road at the junction with Sebright Avenue. The London Road tramway service terminated at Redhill. Trams ran at fifteen minute intervals between 8 a.m. and 11 p.m. on weekdays and Saturdays. Postcard view posted on 23 August 1908.

136 A Red Cross fête was held at the home of Mrs Price-Hughes, Redhill in 1916. This was apparently well attended: framed in the doorway is Sir Edward Elgar, while on the steps can be seen the Dean of Worcester (the Very Reverend W. Moore). Postcard postally used on 4 October 1916. (W. W. Dowty)

137 Worcester College for the Higher Education of the Blind. Snapshot of the headmaster's family. This postcard probably dates from before World War I.

138 A general view of the college from the same period.

139 The frontage of J. F. Mapp, newsagents of No. 71 Sidbury in the summer of 1961.

140 Advertising postcard for the Loch Ryan Hotel. Postally used in the July of 1939. (W. W. Dowty)

141 A further advertising postcard for the Loch Ryan Hotel in Sidbury. (W. W. Dowty)

142 A BSE free environment? The premises of Prosser & Company situated at No. 94 Sidbury. This is the corner of Wylds Lane opposite the defunct Red Lion. Postcard postally used on 19 December 1910.

143 St Michael's church, College Street. This church opened in 1839 but was closed in 1907 when it became the Diocesan Records Office. This ended over 1,000 years of ecclesiastical tradition for the original St Michael's church had been founded in 826. The 1839 building was pulled down in 1962 in order to make way for the Giffard Hotel development. To the left are the premises of the Royal Liver Friendly Society while to the right are the premises of Henry Handley, violin maker. To the right of Handley's premises was the much lamented Lichgate. Circa 1907.

144 The unveiling ceremony of the South African War Memorial on 23 September 1908. On the left can be seen a poster detailing the traffic regulations in force for that day. Over 3,000 county men of the Worcestershire Regiment fought in the Boer War. They served with the First, Second, Third and Fourth Regular Battalions; the First and Second Volunteer Battalions; and the Sixth Militia Battalion. (Percy Parsons)

145 Another view of the unveiling ceremony on a postcard postally used on 10 October 1908.

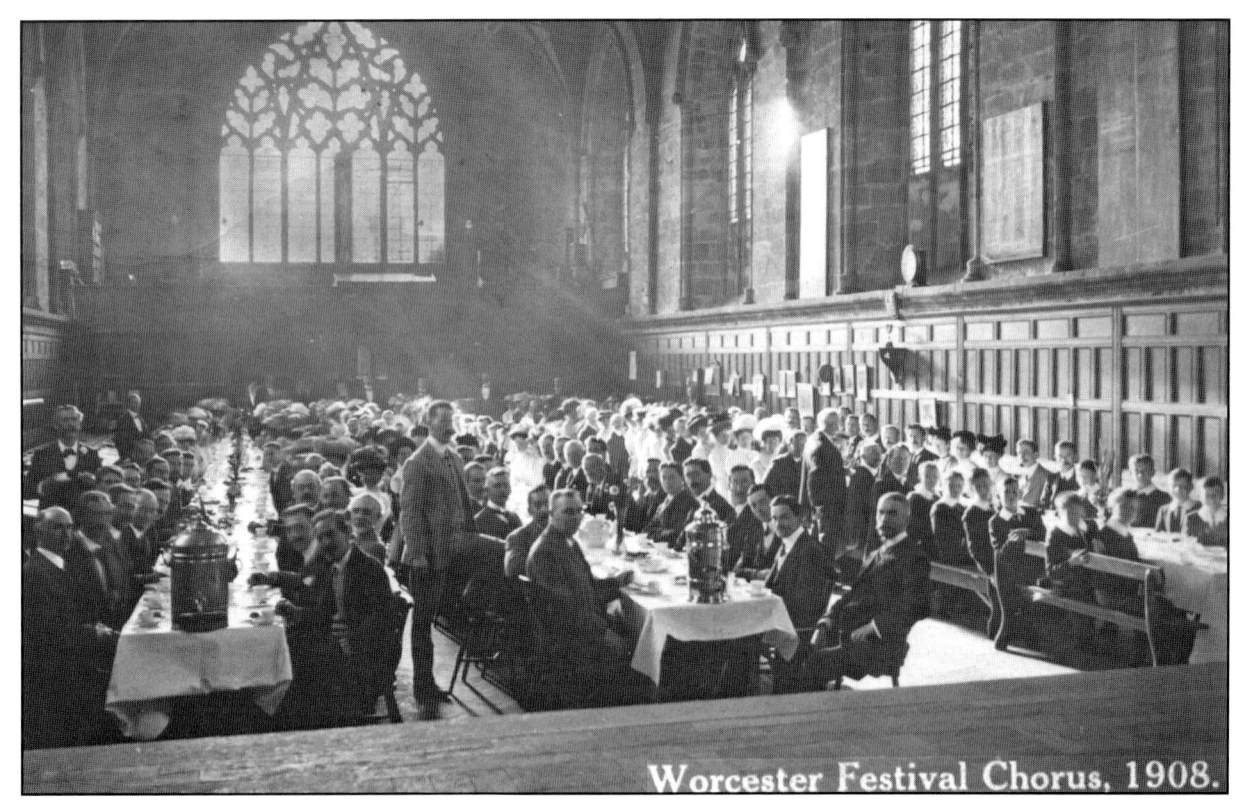

146 Three Choirs Festival of 1908. The chorus dinner was held in the College Hall. The postcard was postally used 10 days after the event on 9 September 1908. Sir Ivor Atkins (the conductor) can be seen standing, while directly behind him sits Doctor G. R. Sinclair. (W. W. Harris)

147 A rather smoky Worcester as seen from the Cathedral tower. In the foreground can be seen the Old Palace, at one time the residence of the bishops of Worcester. It was sold in the 1840s to the Dean and Chapter of Worcester Cathedral for use as the Deanery. Postcard postally used on 21 October 1913. (W. W. Harris)

148, 149 & 150 Three views of the Deanery. Above: the Abbot's Hall, right: the Chapel, below: the Vaulted Hall. The Deanery proved too large for the Dean and became a Church Club and the HQ for the Worcester Diocese. Circa 1906. (W. W. Harris)

151 The bridge as seen from the Deanery gardens. On the left can be seen large haystacks belonging to the farm bordering New Road. (Percy Parsons)

152 An unusual view of South Quay and Copenhagen Street. The two steamers are 'Avonmore' and 'Holt Castle'. Neither of these two steamers survive today although one of their counterparts, the 'Severn Belle', has been restored and now operates as a charter boat on the Thames. It is now called the 'Windsor Belle'. Postally used on 8 September 1908. Printed and published by H. C. Knott, No. 2 Bridge Street.

153 North Quay and the bridge on a photograph taken, purportedly, in 1875. On the right is a typical trow.

154 A similar view possibly taken about 1885. Note the solitary railway wagon on the 'Butts spur' railway line. Behind the wagon is, I assume, the original Old Rectifying House.

155 & 156 The May flood of 1886 (16 ft 11 ins above summer level). This was one of the most devastating floods yet recorded in Worcester being only surpassed by the flood of 1947 (17 ft 9 ins above summer level) and being of a very similar magnitude to the 1770 flood (which was, perhaps, five inches higher). Trapped under the bridge is 'Hastings', a trow belonging to the Droitwich Salt Company Ltd. Both these photographs have postcard backs and, as postcards of this type did not appear until at least 1901, illustrates a policy Bennett & Sons employed of using archive material for their postcard range. (T. Bennett & Sons)

157 Hylton Road in flood during December 1910. Not so impressive as some floods being surpassed in height by at least sixteen other floods in the last 350 years. Postcard sent on 24 December 1910.

158 New Road in flood on 2 June 1924. Only cyclists and pedestrians seem prepared to do battle. This freakish flood (15 ft 9 ins above summer level) wrecked the Three Counties Show being held on Pitchcroft and caused great inconvenience to the residents of the heavily populated areas in Tybridge Street, Hylton Road, Severn Terrace and Diglis. The flood had been proceeded by a month of very heavy rain leaving land in the floodplain of the Severn totally waterlogged.

159 & 160 New Road in flood during March 1947. The 1947 flood was far worse than that of 1924. St John's was literally cut off from the rest of the city as the swollen Teme and Severn broke their banks. Heavy open back lorries ferried people through the floods while a free railway service operated between Foregate Street and Henwick Halt. Burnhams Coaches also operated a free ferry service between the Bull Ring and the bridge. The bus station in Newport Street was completely under water and many of the Midland Red bus services were abandoned. Many people had to be evacuated from their homes and were put up in local hotels and council owned accommodation. (Franklin)

161 The flooded cattle market in March 1947. Facing the market is the now demolished Ewe & Lamb. (Franklin)

162 The view from the Diglis Hotel in March 1947. A good guide to the relative heights of the floods to beset Worcester can be seen nearby at the Cathedral Ferry. Set upon a wall are various stone markers indicating the highest levels recorded by our worst floods. This tradition was started in 1770 when note was also made of the flood of 23 December 1672. This was 10 inches lower than that of 1770. (Franklin)

163 The flooded Severn in the March of 1947.

164 A similar view of the Severn in flood. Date unknown, but possibly the flood of January 1960 (15 ft 11 ins above summer level).

165 A flooded North Parade. To get a drink at the Old Rectifying House a short boat journey and a trip up a ladder are necessary. Date unknown but will be the same year as photo No. 164.

166 Tybridge Street in flood. The view is looking away from the Severn. The premises on the right are those of Johns & Son, St Clement's Works. Date unknown but probably the flood of January 1960.

167 Worcester Cathedral as viewed from the farm that used to exist between the Severn and the Worcestershire County Cricket Club. Postcard sent on 16 March 1909. The writer refers to the bitter cold and snow of the day she experienced in Droitwich and Kings Norton. Kempsey, however, was fine.

168 The pavilion at the county cricket ground. A totally male environment. Cricket at New Road started in 1899 and this photograph probably dates from the early 1900s.

169 An early view of the Worcester Tramways depot situated at the Bull Ring. Date unknown but obviously prior to the electrification of 1904. Both national and local advertisements appear on the tram hoardings.

170 St Johns looking towards the Bromyard Road. Postcard postally used on 13 October 1908. The proprietor of the Angel Hotel was John Appleton. To the left of the Angel are the premises of John Alfred Edwards, cab proprietor and fly proprietor.

171 No. 4 tram heads past St Johns church en route to the Malvern Road terminus situated close to the Brunswick Arms. Between 1904 and 1922 fifteen trams operated the various routes within Worcester. In 1922 an additional two trams were added to the fleet.

172 No. 3 tram pictured at the junction of St John's and Bransford Road. The old building shown is the St John's Ladies College run by the Misses Sessions and Wylde. This is now the site of Our Lady Queen of Peace Primary School and the presbytery of St John's Roman Catholic church. Postcard postally used on 18 July 1904.

173 & 174 Two early views of Malvern Road. Above the view is looking towards the centre of St John's on a postcard sent on 20 July 1908. Below is another view of the southern side of the road with Tower Villa the house nearest the left. The postcard was sent on 22 July 1911. Electric trams never reached this area of the Malvern Road but an omnibus service operated between the Cross and Callow End on a two hourly basis on weekdays (1908). This bus service would have been the main form of transport serving the Powick Asylum and certain buses on Mondays and Thursdays (presumably the main visiting days) ran to and from Asylum Lane.

175 A decaying Hardwick Manor in close-up on a photograph taken by an amateur photographer around 1905. This was the main farm building of what was probably a very large dairy farm. At the time of the Dissolution ownership passed to the Dean and Chapter of Worcester, who were owners of vast tracts of land in this area. The manor house was pulled down in the early 1900s. Great House Road is named after the manor.

177 Opposite page, top. 1886 engraving of Hardwick Manor reproduced on a postcard. (F. S. Bayley)

176 A rare photograph (carte-de-visite) of Hardwick Manor possibly dating back to the 1880s. (Earl)

178 Left: Cleeve House School. This is now the Milk Marque head office.
179 Below: Boughton Park, circa 1904, when the home of Mrs Isaac. This is now the nineteenth hole.

89

180 & 181 River picnic to Worcester. This was a visit from the VAD hospital at Hartlebury in September 1918. Both these photographs are from a superb personal album that belonged to Nurse Stocks. In the photo below - back row, left to right: Pte. Read, Nurse Barber, L/C Liveley, Pte. Coggins, Sister, Commandant, Nurse Joyce Amphlett, Nurse Crowther, Dr. Stuart, Cook, Pte. Wood, Nurse Felton, Nurse Amphlett, Gnr. Lowenthal, Nurse Stocks, Pte. McClean. Centre row: Pte. Coulthard, Pte. Reeve, Nurse Cox, Nurse Marjorie Amphlett. Front row: Pte. Hawkins, L/C Wilson, Pte. Tyler, Pte. Nash, Spr. Crockett, Pte. Armstrong, Pte. Cuthill, Gnr. Woodall, his daughter, Cpl. Fisher, Pte. Baddams. (Iliffe)

182 A river steamer prepares to leave for Holt Fleet. Over the river only the building on the left survives today. In 1908 Littlebury's lists this part of Hylton Road as being home to assorted labourers, a waterman, a boat builder and a french polisher. The Electricity Generating Works, built in 1902, is also discernible towards the right of the photograph. It was important as a source of current for the electrified tramway network. This building was demolished fairly recently.

183 An idyllic river scene. Postcard sent on 12 April 1939.

184 & 185 The royal visit of 28 October 1932. The Prince of Wales, later Edward VIII, flew into Perdiswell airfield for a hectic six hour visit to the 'Faithful City'. His first engagement was at the Guildhall where Worcester's first lady mayor, Miss Diana Ogilvy (above), presented him with a bound 'Address of Welcome'. He officially opened the enlarged (widened from 24ft to 60ft) and modernised Worcester Bridge, the Cripplegate Park (below), and the Nurses Home and other Royal Infirmary extensions. He also made visits to the Worcester Royal Porcelain Works, the Cinderella Shoe factory (J. F. Willis Ltd.) and G. H. Williamsons (Metal Box).

186 Ivor Atkins at work in his study. Atkins attended his first Three Choirs Festival in 1890 and was associated with the event for many years, being made Festival Conductor and Organist of Worcester Cathedral around 1899. He held this appointment for over 50 years. Atkins was a close friend of Sir Edward Elgar and persuaded him to conduct several premieres of his works at the Worcester Three Choirs. Postcard postally used on 15 September 1911. (W. W. Harris)

187 A wedding party outside an unknown public house. (Percy Parsons)

188 Relaxation by the riverside. Location unknown. (Percy Parsons)

189 Working in the countryside. Location unknown. (Percy Parsons)

190 Diabolo was a popular Edwardian pastime that has seen a recent revival. This scene was presumably taken in a Worcester back garden. (A. & G. Colwell)

191 Playing doctors and nurses at an unknown local fête. (A. & G. Colwell)

192 Williamson's ladies football team photographed at St George's Lane in 1917. They played the Heenan & Froude ladies team. Back row, left to right: Mr. F. Wells (trainer), Mrs E. Dean (lady assistant), -?-, Miss Lawrance, Cook, Yapp, Underhill, Roberts, F. Sutton (lady assistant), M. J. Rotheram (first aid). Front row: Miss P. Wood, Sandles, Irons, Dixon, Robinson.

193 Nurses take time out for afternoon tea. This photograph was most probably taken at Newtown Hospital. (Percy Parsons)

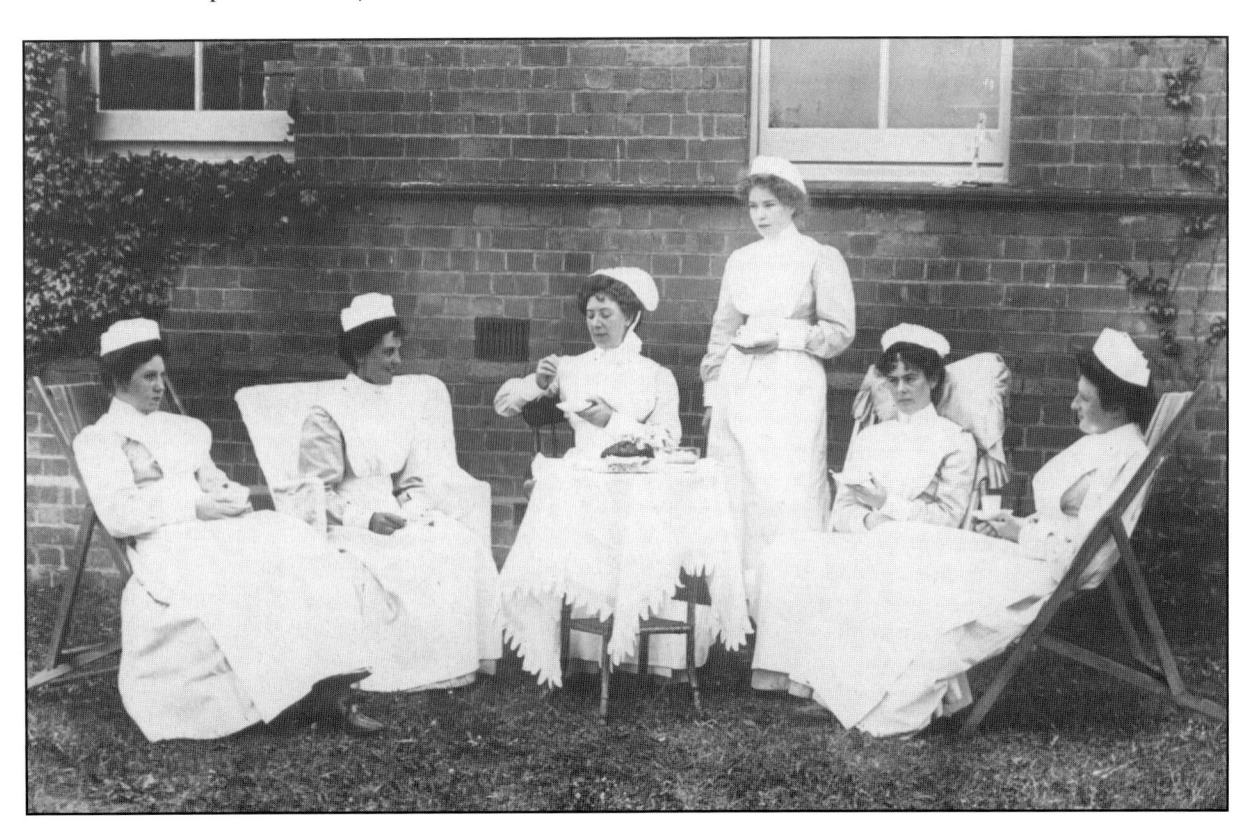

194 Worcester's well-known Vesta Tilley. The above postcard publicises her first appearance at The Palace Theatre in London. Also on the bill were Princess Trixie, Little Tich, The Juggling McBans, Chirgwin and Miss Margaret Cooper.

195 Vesta Tilley in golfing action on the Ravenscliffe Golf Links, Bradford. Postcard postally used on 12 March 1907.

196 A schoolboy and cycle (E. J. Parsons collection). SMS could stand for St Martins School. (Max Fischer)

197 A Grammar School pupil. Postcard postally used on 8 November 1910.

198 A racing pigeon not guilty of deception! C. E. Watts was a hardware dealer.

"DECEPTION."
Blue Cheq. Hen, 782/12 H.P.

Flown 1912, Wickwar. 1913, Guernsey. 1914, Guernsey and Marennes. 1915, Untrained. 1916, Bath. 1917, Bath. 1918, Weymouth. 1919, 4th Guernsey. 1920, 1st Guernsey, St. John's F.C. 1st, W.U.F.C. 1st, W. & D.F.C. and special 7th Fed. and Pool, velocity 896. 1,882 Birds. 1st Marennes in three Clubs, 1st Fed. and 1st Midland Counties Combine 2/6 Pool and H.P. special, beating next competitor by over 100 yards per minute.

Bred and Flown by C. E. WATTS, 24, Friar Street, Worcester.

> THE OLD FIRM
>
> Tours, Contract and Private Hire
>
> 'Phone 2008
> Proprietor
> C. J. MARKS
>
> TRAVEL BY ROAD
> You've Tried the Rest — Now Try the Best!!
> **BLUE COACH SERVICES**
> LONDON ROAD, WORCESTER

199 Advertising postcard for the Blue Coach Services run by the well known C. J. Marks. The earliest Marks' owned vehicles appear in photo No. 232.

200 Advertising postcard used by Holtham & Co., No. 4 Corn Market to bring attention to their range of palatine cakes & meals. Postcard postally used on 31 December 1906.

A SPLENDID SHORTHORN HEIFER.

99

201 'Life's a drag' - well, for these horses it certainly was! J. L. Larkworthy, agricultural engineers, were based at Lowesmoor. Their drags were described as follows: 'These drags possess the advantage over the ordinary duck footed drags in being mounted on wheels, which permit of their being so regulated in work as to go go deeper or shallower as required. Made in three sizes - for two, three or four horses.' Circa 1910.

202 A selection of Firkin's motoring gloves on a representatives postcard addressed to W. H. Richards, ironmonger of Ludlow. Firkins were based at No. 9 Foregate Street. Circa 1904.

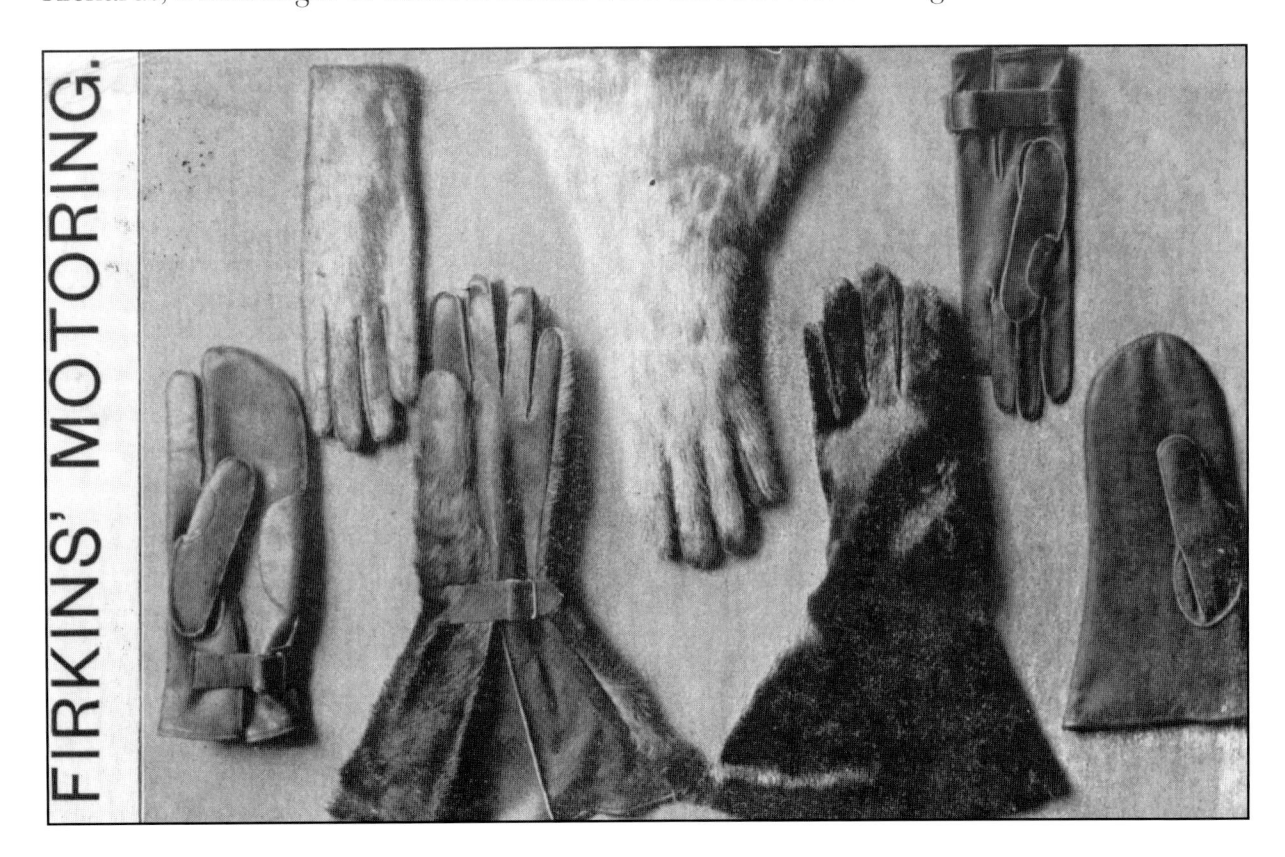

203 Election for the City Auditors held in the Guildhall. Date unknown but probably around 1910. (Percy Parsons)

204 A typical small shopkeeper's premises. Perhaps a recognisable location? The Theatre Royal's annual pantomime was to be 'Aladdin' presented by Fred Clements. The first performance was to be on Boxing Day.

101

205 The Tudor Girls Club at an unknown location in Worcester. (A. & G. Colwell)

206 St. Clement's scout troop in the school playground. The scout leader on the left is probably W. J. Fiddler of Cole Hill who took the photograph, used it as a postcard, and also submitted it for publication in the Berrows Illustrated Supplement of 20 May 1911.

207 Worcester traders at Evesham. S. J. Winkle & Sons were based at the Market Hall & Shambles, Worcester but evidently took their wares to Evesham market and other local markets on a regular basis. The firm of Pratleys, founded in the 1870s by Richard Pratley, was known as Winkle when Richard's widow married John Winkle. After his early death she reverted to her former married name. (P. Hutchison)

208 An electric tram especially decorated for Lifeboat Saturday. Worcester had a long tradition of raising money in aid of lifeboats. Circa 1909. (T. Bennett & Sons)

209 'Jack & Jill' pantomime at the Theatre Royal, 1 January 1923. This was an annual event.

210 & 211 Edwardian advertising postcards for the Worcester Theatre Royal. Below left: 'The Count of Luxembourg'. Below right: 'Sergeant Brue'. Other typical plays at that time included 'The Eternal City', 'Remnant', 'A Waltz Dream', 'Our Miss Gibbs', 'The Coastguard's Daughter' and 'When Knights were Bold'.

212 Old cottages at Bevere Green. Postcard postally used on 10 July 1907. These cottages still exist albeit in slightly different form. (Attributed to Pitt & Son)

213 Bevere Green in winter splendour. Postcard postally used on 7 July 1907. The above cottages would be in the vicinity of the photographer's tripod (probably Pitt & Son).

214 Bevere Green as perceived by one romance-minded young lady in Edwardian times.

215 Porter's Mill on an Edwardian postcard not postally used until 1956. Elizabeth I is reputed to have slept here. (W. W. Harris)

216 St Nicholas church, Warndon. This photograph was taken prior to 1909 when renovation work was carried out. Set amidst very rural surroundings in Edwardian times this church now overlooks the developments of modern day Worcester and is a small oasis of relative calm. However, its importance as a church serving the local community has been considerably enhanced.

217 Trotshill is now firmly entrenched within the confines of Worcester and the remaining cottages no longer have such tranquil surroundings.

218 Trotshill Lane showing Trotshill Farm and the old grain store built on staddlestones. This was known locally as 'the old apple store'. The farmer in 1908 was Alfred Bevan Purnell who also farmed the Warndon Farm. (W. W. Harris)

219 Spetchley still manages to avoid the clutches of Worcester and this Edwardian view is little changed today. On the left is the entrance to the now refurbished cemetery. Spetchley Park and Spetchley church are behind the wall on the right. (W. W. Harris)

220 Whittington village. This view has not changed greatly. The population of this village, now virtually engulfed by the sprawling city, was 429 in 1901. (Pitt & Son)

221 Swan Inn, Whittington. The licensee in 1908 was Frederick Gossage who boasted of 'home-brewed ales, wines, spirits and cigars of the finest quality. Good stabling. Accommodation for cyclists.' (Pitt & Son)

222 Whittington School. Postcard postally used on 24 July 1908. (Pitt & Son)

223 The Berkeley Knot, Sneachill, White Ladies Aston. A superb photograph possibly dating from around 1920 when Herbert Henry Young was the licensee. He was also licensee in 1908 when the hostelry was called the Crown. Another change of name for this pub was perhaps inevitable when it was refurbished recently. Not too memorable I'm afraid. However, perhaps if you think of a bird singing in Berkeley Square the reason for the change of name may become apparent.

224 Norton Barracks pictured in the Edwardian period. This was the headquarters of the Worcestershire Regiment, but is now a housing development. (W. W. Harris)

225 A demonstration omnibus pictured outside Norton Barracks on election day. The postcard being postally used on 27 January 1910. The omnibus was built by Scammell & Nephew of London.

226 Norton Junction station on a postcard postally used on 29 August 1932. The station, renamed Norton Halt in 1959, was closed on 3 January 1966. (Published by M. E. Harber, Norton Post Office)

227 Interior view of the church of St James, Norton, circa 1906. The church served a population of 807 (including 199 in the barracks) in 1901. (W. W. Harris)

228 Old bridge, Powick. This shows the cluster of old mill buildings that existed on this site until about 1924. Mills had thrived on this site since at least the eleventh century and during the nineteenth century a total of seven waterwheels operated four mills at this spot on the Teme: Hadley's Corn Mill, Chamberlains' China Clay Mill, a malt dressing mill and a clover dressing mill. A lady who died in 1914 is said to remember the times when donkeys pulled river barges to the Powick mills.

229 New bridge, Powick. In the background is the Electric Lighting Station for the City of Worcester which opened in 1894.

230 Powick Asylum. Postcard postally used on 2 May 1904.

231 Powick Mental Hospital on a much more recent postcard. The hospital closed a few years ago and now, like Norton Barracks, has become an area of new housing development.

232 An outing from the Red Lion, Powick. Alfred Rodgman was the licensee at the time of this photograph which probably dates from around 1920. The buses shown are two of the first owned by Cecil Marks, the founder of the well known 'Marks's Buses'.

233 Another view of the Red Lion on a postcard postally used 6 August 1939. (Published by J. A. Knott, Powick Post Office)

234 Upper Wick. Postcard postally used on 4 November 1937.

235 Upper Wick (both Nos. 234 & 235 were postcards published for J. H. Chalke, Rushwick Post Office).

SUBSCRIBERS

This is book no. 81 of 250 numbered copies.

1. Alan B. Anderson
2. F.R. Appleford
3. Diane & David Armstrong
4. Mrs B. Badger
5. Mrs P. Badham
6. Councillor David Barlow
7. John C. Barnes
8. D.M. Barwell
9. Mrs D.M. Bayliss
10. Mr Geoff Beasant
11. Mrs S.J. Bennett
12. Bill Berry
13. Janette Birbeck
14. Geoff Bird
15. William Bourne
16. Constance Bowcott
17. L.J. Bowkett
18. Mr H.W. Bramwell
19. Mrs K. M. Brannen
20. John Brettell
21. Mr & Mrs A. Brookes
22. M.A. Browne
23. R.E. Bruton
24. Roger Bunting
25. Charles Caldicott
26. Christine Champken
27. Jonathan Chilton
28. Roy Ciric
29. Phyllis & Ern Clarke
30. Mr R.G. Clews
31. E. Phillip Cole
32. C.L. Connell
33. Ernest J. Cook
34. Mrs J. Crowe
35. George P. Crowley
36. Mr J. Cruttenden
37. Ken Crump
38. Mr Ian Dandridge
39. Alan Davies
40. Mr Des Davies
41. Christine Bannister
42. Colin Anthony Day
43. A.H. Deakin
44. Reg Dovey
45. Michael Dowty
46. Mr L.A. Drinkwater
47. Mr S.P. Drinkwater
48. Brian Druce
49. L.A. Drury
50. Beryl Dursley
51. Mrs A. Dutfield
52. Roy Ellis
53. Mr John E. Evans
54. Roy & Gill Everett
55. Mr M. Ewins
56. Mr M. Ewins
57. Mr Neville Fairbairn
58. Dr A.G. Fielding
59. William L. Foley
60. Mrs E.J. Fowler
61. Brian Garrett
62. R.E. German
63. Roy & Shirley Gilmour
64. Mrs Adreine Godfrey
65. Mr John Godfrey
66. Graham & Sheila
67. Stuart Harvey Griffiths
68. Michael Grundy
69. Nelson Roper
70. Reg Smart
71. Kathleen Broom
72. Mrs C.G. Hand
73. Cynthia B. Harding
74. June & Dennis Harford
75. Ella Harris
76. Mr & Mrs G. Harris
77. Grahame Harris
78. L. Harris
79. Mike & Lynda Hawkins
80. George & Edna Haywood
81. Russell & Patti Haywood
82. Jill & Tony King
83. V. Hemingway
84. Graham Henderson
85. Mrs E. Henney
86. N.J. Hinton
87. Brian Hodgkins
88. Colin Holmes
89. Mr R.C. Howell
90. Mary Hyde
91. Astor Innes
92. I.M. Jarvis

93	Ron Jaynes	144	Paul & Debbie Murton
94	Mr A. Jenkins	145	Susan Nash
95	Mr Ivor Jenkins	146	Anthony John Nicholls
96	B.J. Jerrum	147	Mr K. Paterson
97	M.R. Jerrum	148	Mr D.G. Payne
98	Mr & Mrs D.J. Jinks	149	Peter Perks
99	Roger Gaywood Fisher	150	David C. Phillips
100	Mrs G.H. Jones	151	Mrs J. Phillips
101	Ray Jones	152	Jean Pinches
102	Ray & Brenda Jones	153	Mr & Mrs R. Powell
103	Mr R.S. Jones	154	S.J. Pratley
104	Brian Keogh	155	E.G. Preece
105	Peter Kimberley	156	Mrs A.E. Price
106	Bill Kite	157	Eric E. Price
107	Les Kite	158	Dennis & Rose Pugh
108	Mr G.W. Lamb	159	Mrs J. Ratcliffe
109	Roger P. Lambourne	160	Mr K. Ratcliffe
110	Les & Joan Lampitt	161	Terry Ramsden
111	Mrs Josey Leader	162	Robert Rayers
112	Simon & Tracey Leader	163	Dave Rice
113	Ken Lee	164	P.B. Richardson
114	Mrs W.L. Lee	165	Mr & Mrs Laurence Rodgers
115	George T. Lewis	166	John Rouse
116	Mrs Jean Lewis	167	Mr David Ruff
117	Mrs Jean Lewis	168	Graham Ruff
118	Jon Lewis	169	Mrs J. Salt
119	Mr K.C. Lewis	170	Mrs M.A. Sayers
120	Margaret R. Lloyd	171	Louis Schroeder
121	Mr W.J. Lowe	172	F.C. Shapcott
122	Heather Magee	173	Norman Sharpley
123	W.J.D. Malsbury	174	P.A. Shearman
124	Mr & Mrs G.W. Mann	175	Mavis Sarfras
125	Steve Mann	176	Gerald Shirvington
126	Irene M. Mapp	177	Ron Shuard
127	Irene M. Mapp	178	Francis Mary Simmonds
128	Mr & Mrs J. Marchant	179	Malcolm Simpkins
129	Mr & Mrs R. Marchant	180	Brian Skyrme
130	Denis Edward Margrett	181	Colin Skyrme
131	William Masters	182	Mrs R. Small
132	Philip J. Maylor	183	Sylvia Snape
133	Raymond Mayne	184	Anthony Squire DBA
134	Arthur Meigh	185	Mr C.W. Stenson
135	Mrs H.I. Moore	186	Mr C.W. Stenson
136	Anon	187	Mavis & Derick Stephens
137	Anon	188	Tim Sherwood
138	Anon	189	David A. Taylor
139	Audrey, John, Sam & Phil Moran	190	Edward E. Taylor
140	Mrs V. Morris	191	Mrs L. England
141	Mrs V. Morris	192	Mr & Mrs T. Taylor
142	Ken & Ruth Patrick	193	Mrs V.M. Taylor
143	John Murphy	194	Vaughan & Janet Thomas

195	Mr & Mrs David Thomson	223	Worcester U3A
196	Mr & Mrs J. Tolley	224	Worcester U3A
197	D.A. Walker	225	Worcester U3A
198	Eric Ernest Webb	226	Worcester U3A
199	Mr K. Weston	227	Worcester U3A
200	B.J. Whelan	228	Worcester U3A
201	Tony Williams	229	Worcester U3A
202	Doreen Willis	230	Worcester U3A
203	Mr J. Willis	231	Worcester U3A
204	John Willis	232	Worcester U3A
205	Paul Willis	233	F.W. Rayers
206	Mrs B.E. Wilton	234	Mr T. Wallcroft
207	Mrs L.J. Wilton	235	Marjorie Harris
208	Malcolm & Ann Woodward	236	Annette Leach
209	Mr & Mrs Anthony North	237	
210	Worcestershire Record Office	238	
211	A.W. Wright	239	
212	Mrs D.R. Wright	240	
213	Mr P.R. Young	241	
214	Anon	242	
215	Anon	243	
216	Anon	244	
217	Anon	245	
218	Maurice Hutt	246	
219	F. Hughes	247	
220	Tom Ditchfield	248	
221	Mrs G. Corbett	249	
222	Margaret Fernyhough	250	

Remaining subscribers unlisted. Books beyond No. 250 are not numbered.